THE ART OF WORLD DOMINANCE

Support Systems

and

Fear Systems

By

Melvin Prince Johnakin

The Art of World Dominance, Support Systems and Fear Systems

Copyright 2024 by Melvin Prince Johnakin

All rights reserved. No part of this publication may be reproduced, distributed, or transmitted in any form or by any means, including photocopying, recording, or other electronic or mechanical methods, without the prior written permission of the publisher, except in the case of brief quotations embodied in critical reviews and certain other noncommercial uses permitted by copyright law.

Although the author and publisher have made every effort to ensure that the information in this book was correct at press time, the author and publisher do not assume and hereby disclaim any liability to any party for any loss, damage, or disruption caused by errors or omissions, whether such errors or omissions result from negligence, accident, or any other cause. Adherence to all applicable laws and regulations, including international, federal, state, and local governing professional licensing, business practices, advertising, and all other aspects of doing business in the US, Canada or any other jurisdiction is the sole responsibility of the reader and consumer.

Neither the author nor the publisher assumes any responsibility or liability whatsoever on behalf of the consumer or reader of this material. Any perceived slight of any individual or organization is purely unintentional.

The resources in this book are provided for informational purposes only and should not be used to replace the specialized training and professional judgment of a health care or mental health care professional. Neither the author nor the publisher can be held responsible for the use of the information provided within this book. Please always consult a trained professional before making any decision regarding treatment of yourself or others

Forward

It is with great humility and a sense of responsibility that I have been granted the honor of composing the forward for this seminal work. The exploration of race, societal support structures, and the psychological conditioning that shapes disparities in confidence and fear is a crucial undertaking in our collective quest for a more just and equitable world. The author's dedication to unraveling the complexities of these intersecting forces is a testament to their commitment to advancing the discourse on race relations and systemic bias.

In our contemporary society, the impact of race on individual experiences and opportunities cannot be overstated. The interplay between societal structures and psychological conditioning is a significant determinant in shaping the life trajectories of individuals from different racial backgrounds. By delving into these intricate dynamics, the author invites us to confront uncomfortable truths and challenge prevailing narratives that perpetuate inequity.

The Importance of addressing these issues cannot be overstated. To create a more equitable world, we must understand the systems that perpetuate disparities in confidence and fear. We must be willing to engage in difficult conversations and take meaningful action to dismantle oppressive structures. Only by acknowledging and confronting these realities can we begin to lay the groundwork for a future where every individual, regardless of race, can thrive unencumbered by the weight of systemic bias.

As you embark on this journey through the pages of this book, I urge you to approach the material with an open mind and a willingness to confront uncomfortable truths. It is only through this introspection and critical examination that we can collectively work towards a more just and equitable world for all.

Introduction

In the intricate tapestry of human society, the differential social conditioning of individuals based on race has profound and far-reaching implications. This book seeks to unravel the complex web of factors that underpin disparities in confidence and fear among individuals of different racial backgrounds. At the heart of this exploration lies the thesis that the differential treatment of white and black individuals within societal systems has a direct influence on their emotional resilience and, consequently, their ability to navigate the world with confidence or to grapple with fear and vulnerability.

The historical context and contemporary manifestations of these systems weave a narrative that is as compelling as it is troubling. The legacies of oppression, discrimination, and marginalization have left an indelible mark on the lived experiences of individuals from marginalized racial groups. Conversely, the privileges and advantages afforded to individuals from dominant racial groups have bolstered their confidence and resilience within societal structures.

We are setting the stage for a deeper exploration of these intersecting forces. By examining the historical roots of these disparities and shining a light on their contemporary manifestations, we lay the groundwork for a comprehensive understanding of the systemic barriers that hinder the full realization of human potential. Through this exploration, we aim to challenge the status quo and provoke thoughtful reflection on how we can collectively work towards a more equitable and just society for all.

Acknowledgments

I am deeply indebted to the scholars, experts, historians, psychologists, sociologists, and activists whose invaluable insights have informed the pages of this book. Their dedication to advancing knowledge and social justice has enriched the discourse presented here, and I am profoundly grateful for their contributions.

Additionally, I extend my heartfelt appreciation to my friends, family, and colleagues whose unwavering support and constructive feedback have been instrumental in shaping the development of this work. Their encouragement and thoughtful engagement have been a source of strength and inspiration throughout the writing process.

To the experts and scholars whose research and wisdom form the foundation of this exploration, I express my deepest gratitude. Your tireless dedication to unraveling the complexities of race relations and systemic bias has been a guiding light, illuminating the path towards greater understanding and societal change.

I would also like to acknowledge the historians whose work has provided critical insights into the historical context of racial dynamics and the enduring impact of past injustices on present-day realities. Their scholarship has been instrumental in shaping the historical framework that underpins the discussions within this book.

The Invaluable contributions of psychologists and sociologists cannot be overstated. Their expertise in understanding the human mind and the intricate fabric of societal structures has enriched the analysis presented in these pages, providing a nuanced perspective on the psychological conditioning that drives disparities in confidence and fear.

Furthermore, the tireless efforts of activists who have dedicated their lives to advocating for racial justice and equity deserve our utmost appreciation. Their courage, resilience, and unwavering commitment to change have served as an inspiration and a call to action for all those who seek a more just and equitable world.

Finally, to my friends, family, and colleagues, I extend my heartfelt thanks. Your unwavering support, encouragement, and understanding have been the bedrock upon which this endeavor has been built. Your willingness to engage in meaningful dialogue and offer constructive feedback has been invaluable, and I am deeply grateful for your presence on this journey.

In closing, I am profoundly thankful to all those who have contributed to the realization of this work. It is my hope that the discussions within these pages will serve as a catalyst for meaningful change, sparking dialogue, introspection, and action towards a world where every individual can thrive free from the constraints of systemic bias and injustice.

Chapter 1

The Foundations of Dominance

The historical roots of racial dominance are deeply intertwined with the legacies of colonialism and slavery, creating enduring patterns of white confidence and black fear. To understand the contemporary dynamics of race and power, it is essential to delve into the historical forces that have shaped and perpetuated these patterns. This chapter will explore the origins of racial dominance, tracing its development from the era of colonial expansion to the institution of slavery, and examining how these historical forces continue to reverberate in the present day.

Colonialism and the Construction of Racial Hierarchy
The seeds of racial dominance were sown during the era of European colonial expansion, as explorers and conquerors ventured into new territories and encountered indigenous populations. The encounter between European colonizers and native peoples laid the groundwork for the construction of racial hierarchies, as the former sought to assert their dominance over the latter. The development of racial categories and the assignment of value and worth based on race became central to the colonial project, as Europeans justified their subjugation and exploitation of indigenous peoples through the dehumanization and othering of non-white populations.

The establishment of racial hierarchies served to consolidate the power and authority of the colonial rulers, providing a rationale for the subjugation and exploitation of indigenous peoples. This process not only entrenched the dominance of the colonizers but also laid the groundwork for the racialization of power dynamics, as whiteness became synonymous with authority and superiority, while non-white populations were relegated to positions of subordination and inferiority.

Slavery and the Enshrinement of Racial Subjugation

The transatlantic slave trade further entrenched patterns of racial dominance, as millions of Africans were forcibly transported to the Americas to toil under brutal conditions on plantations and in other labor-intensive industries. The institution of slavery was predicated on the dehumanization of black people, who were treated as property and denied basic rights and freedoms. The exploitation of African labor underpinned the economic prosperity of European colonies and, later, the United States, while reinforcing the notion of racial hierarchy and the inherent inferiority of black individuals.

Slavery not only served as an economic institution but also played a pivotal role in shaping social and cultural attitudes towards race. The brutal and dehumanizing conditions of slavery served to instill fear among black populations, as they were subjected to violence, oppression, and the constant threat of separation from their families. Meanwhile, the institution of slavery bolstered the confidence of white slave owners and society at large, as the subjugation of black individuals became normalized and entrenched within the fabric of society.

The Legacy of Colonialism and Slavery

The legacies of colonialism and slavery continue to reverberate in contemporary society, shaping the dynamics of race and power in profound ways. The enduring impact of these historical forces is evident in the persistence of racial inequality, institutionalized discrimination, and the perpetuation of racial stereotypes and biases. The patterns of white confidence and black fear that were established during the era of colonialism and slavery continue to manifest in present-day power dynamics, as systemic structures and societal attitudes reinforce racial dominance and subjugation.

Conclusion

The foundations of racial dominance were established through the historical forces of colonialism and slavery, which constructed and perpetuated patterns of white confidence and black fear. The legacies of these historical dynamics continue to shape contemporary society, underscoring the enduring impact of historical oppression and the urgent need for addressing racial inequality and dismantling systems of racial dominance. By recognizing the historical roots of racial hierarchy and the enduring patterns of white confidence and black fear, society can begin to confront the pervasive impact of these legacies and work towards meaningful change.

Moving forward, it is imperative to engage in conversations about race, power, and privilege, acknowledging the ways in which historical forces continue to shape contemporary realities. This necessitates a commitment to dismantling systemic racism, addressing disparities in access to resources and opportunities, and challenging entrenched attitudes and biases. By centering the experiences and perspectives of marginalized communities, society can work towards creating a more equitable and just future for all.

Furthermore, it is essential to critically examine and redefine the structures and institutions that perpetuate racial dominance. This includes reforming criminal justice systems, addressing disparities in healthcare and education, and promoting inclusive policies that uplift marginalized communities. Additionally, fostering diverse and inclusive representations in media, arts, and education can challenge prevailing narratives and promote a more nuanced understanding of race and history.

Ultimately, addressing the foundations of racial dominance requires a multifaceted approach that encompasses social, political, and cultural dimensions. By interrogating the historical roots of racial hierarchy and actively working to dismantle systems of oppression, society can strive towards a more equitable and inclusive future. This necessitates a commitment to ongoing education, advocacy, and allyship, as well as a willingness to confront discomfort and challenge the status quo.

In conclusion, the historical roots of racial dominance, stemming from colonialism and slavery, have left an indelible mark on contemporary society. Understanding and acknowledging these historical forces is essential for confronting and addressing racial inequality. By actively working to dismantle systems of racial dominance, society can strive towards a more just and equitable future, where the patterns of white confidence and black fear are replaced by a shared commitment to equality and justice for all.

Chapter 2

Teaching Confidence

Confidence is a crucial attribute that shapes an individual's ability to navigate the world and assert their place within it. In the context of race, confidence is not evenly distributed, and the mechanisms through which it is instilled in white youth are deeply intertwined with social, familial, and educational systems. This chapter will explore the ways in which confidence is taught and cultivated among white youth, examining the social structures, familial dynamics, and educational environments that contribute to the development of confidence. Through examples and case studies, we will seek to understand the complex interplay of factors that shape white youth's sense of confidence and the implications of this phenomenon within the broader context of racial dynamics.

Social Structures and Cultural Reinforcement

Confidence among white youth is often reinforced and cultivated within broader social structures that perpetuate racial hierarchies. From a young age, white children are often surrounded by representations of success, power, and authority that reflect and affirm their racial identity. Media, popular culture, and historical narratives frequently center and celebrate the achievements and contributions of white individuals, contributing to a sense of entitlement and assurance.

Moreover, white children often benefit from social networks and opportunities that provide them with affirming experiences and reinforce their sense of self-worth. Access to extracurricular activities, mentorship, and leadership opportunities within their communities further bolster their confidence and sense of capability. These experiences, often taken for granted, contribute to a pervasive sense of entitlement and self-assuredness among white youth.

Familial Dynamics and Privilege

Within the family unit, white youth are often socialized into a world that affirms their worth and capabilities. Their parents and caregivers, who themselves may have benefited from societal privilege, impart a sense of confidence and self-assuredness through their actions, attitudes, and expectations. White children are often encouraged to express themselves, take risks, and assert their opinions, fostering a sense of entitlement and agency.

Furthermore, familial resources and support often provide white youth with a safety net that allows them to navigate the world with a greater sense of security and assurance. Economic stability, access to quality education, and familial networks all contribute to a sense of confidence and optimism about their prospects.

Educational Environments and Affirmation

Educational settings play a significant role in shaping white youth's confidence. Research indicates that white students often receive more positive feedback and encouragement from teachers, which can contribute to their sense of self-worth and confidence in their abilities. Additionally, the curriculum and teaching materials frequently center on narratives and perspectives that affirm and validate the experiences of white students, reinforcing their sense of belonging and value within the educational environment.

Furthermore, white students often benefit from a lack of stigma associated with their racial identity within educational settings. They are less likely to face stereotypes or negative assumptions based on their race, allowing them to navigate academic and social spaces with greater ease and confidence.

Case Studies and Examples

To illustrate these dynamics, we can examine specific case studies and examples that highlight the ways in which confidence is cultivated among white youth. For instance, we could explore the experiences of white students in predominantly white schools versus those in diverse educational settings, examining how their sense of confidence is shaped by the racial dynamics of their environment. Additionally, we could analyze the impact of family wealth and social capital on the development of confidence among white youth, drawing on real-life examples to elucidate the ways in which privilege contributes to a sense of entitlement and assurance.

Conclusion, the cultivation of confidence among white youth is deeply embedded within social, familial, and educational systems that affirm their sense of entitlement and self-assuredness. By examining the interplay of these factors, we gain insight into the ways in which racial privilege contributes to the development of confidence and its implications within the broader context of racial dynamics.

Understanding the mechanisms through which confidence is taught to white youth is essential for addressing the disparities in confidence and self-assuredness that exist along racial lines. By critically examining the societal structures, familial dynamics, and educational environments that contribute to the cultivation of confidence, we can work towards fostering a more equitable and inclusive society.

Moving forward, it is imperative to address the systemic factors that perpetuate disparities in confidence and self-esteem among youth from different racial backgrounds. This includes reevaluating educational practices to ensure that all students receive equitable support and affirmation, promoting diverse and inclusive representations in media and popular culture, and actively challenging societal narratives that reinforce racial hierarchies.

Furthermore, it is essential to engage in conversations about privilege and power, fostering an awareness of the ways in which racial dynamics shape individual experiences and opportunities. By centering the voices and experiences of marginalized communities, society can work towards dismantling systems of privilege and creating a more just and equitable future for all youth.

By critically examining the social, familial, and educational systems that instill confidence in white youth, we can begin to address the pervasive impact of racial privilege and work towards creating a more inclusive and affirming environment for all young individuals, regardless of their racial background.

Chapter 3

The Anatomy of Fear

Fear is a powerful and pervasive force that shapes the lived experiences of black individuals within the context of systemic racism. This chapter will provide an in-depth analysis of how fear is taught to black individuals through the mechanisms of systemic racism, with a specific focus on the impact of police brutality and economic disenfranchisement. By examining the multifaceted nature of fear within the context of racial dynamics, we seek to shed light on the ways in which systemic injustices perpetuate a climate of fear and insecurity among black communities.

Police Brutality and the Policing of Black Bodies

One of the most visible and visceral manifestations of fear within the black community is the pervasive threat of police brutality. Black individuals, particularly men, are disproportionately targeted and subjected to violence and harassment by law enforcement agencies. The historical legacy of policing black bodies as a means of social control, rooted in the era of slavery and Jim Crow segregation, continues to reverberate in contemporary interactions between black individuals and law enforcement.

The prevalence of high-profile cases of police brutality, often captured on video and disseminated through media channels, contributes to a climate of fear and mistrust within black communities. The repeated exposure to these traumatic events, coupled with the lack of accountability within the criminal justice system, instills a profound sense of vulnerability and apprehension among black individuals, shaping their interactions with authority and the broader society.

Economic Disenfranchisement and Structural Inequity

In addition to the threat of physical violence, black individuals experience fear as a result of enduring economic disenfranchisement and structural inequity. Systemic barriers to employment, housing, and educational opportunities contribute to a pervasive sense of insecurity and uncertainty within black communities. The intergenerational impact of discriminatory policies, such as redlining and unequal access to economic resources, perpetuates cycles of poverty and marginalization, fostering a climate of fear and precarity.

Moreover, the disproportionate impact of economic hardship on black communities intersects with the broader social and political landscape, exacerbating feelings of powerlessness and disenfranchisement. The fear of economic instability, coupled with the lack of access to resources and opportunities, contributes to a sense of hopelessness and vulnerability among black individuals, shaping their perceptions of the world and their place within it.

Intersectional Analysis and the Compounding Effects of Fear

It is essential to recognize that the experiences of fear within black communities are often shaped by intersecting factors, including gender, sexuality, and other dimensions of identity. Black women, for example, contend with unique forms of fear and insecurity, stemming from the pervasive threat of gender-based violence and the intersecting impact of racial and gender discrimination. Similarly, LGBTQ+ individuals within black communities face heightened fears related to discrimination, violence, and social exclusion, compounding the effects of systemic racism.

By engaging in an intersectional analysis, we can gain a more comprehensive understanding of the multifaceted nature of fear within black communities and the ways in which systemic injustices intersect to create a climate of pervasive insecurity and apprehension.

Conclusion

The anatomy of fear within black communities is deeply intertwined with the mechanisms of systemic racism, encompassing the pervasive threat of police brutality, economic disenfranchisement, and intersecting forms of discrimination. By critically examining the ways in which fear is taught to black individuals through systemic injustices, we can begin to address the enduring impact of racial dynamics and work towards fostering a more just and equitable society.

Moving forward, it is imperative to address the systemic factors that perpetuate fear and insecurity within black communities. This includes reforming law enforcement practices to combat police brutality and promote accountability, as well as addressing the economic disparities that contribute to the perpetuation of fear and precarity. Additionally, initiatives aimed at dismantling systemic racism and promoting equity should center the voices and experiences of black individuals, fostering an inclusive and affirming environment that acknowledges the pervasive impact of fear and insecurity.

Furthermore, it is essential to engage in conversations about privilege, power, and the intersectional nature of fear within black communities. By centering the experiences of marginalized individuals and amplifying their voices, society can work towards dismantling systems of oppression and creating a more just and equitable future for all individuals, regardless of their racial background.

The anatomy of fear within black communities is deeply rooted in the mechanisms of systemic racism, encompassing the pervasive threat of police brutality, economic disenfranchisement, and intersecting forms of discrimination. By critically examining the multifaceted nature of fear, we can begin to address the enduring impact of racial dynamics and work towards fostering a more just and equitable society that affirms the experiences and dignity of all individuals.

Chapter 4

Media Portrayals and Perception

Media representations play a significant role in shaping societal perceptions of race and reinforcing racial stereotypes. This chapter will examine how media portrayals contribute to the reinforcement of racial stereotypes, which in turn encourage confidence in white individuals and instill fear in black individuals. By analyzing the ways in which media narratives shape perceptions of race, we can gain insight into the profound impact of these representations on the dynamics of confidence and fear within society.

Reinforcement of White Confidence

Media representations often affirm and perpetuate narratives that reinforce confidence in white individuals. In film, television, and advertising, white characters are frequently depicted as protagonists, leaders, and heroes, reinforcing a narrative of competence, authority, and desirability. These portrayals contribute to a sense of entitlement and self-assuredness among white audiences, affirming their place within the societal hierarchy.

Furthermore, media representations often perpetuate a standard of beauty and success that aligns with white norms, further affirming the confidence of white individuals. By centering and celebrating white experiences, achievements, and perspectives, media narratives contribute to the normalization and perpetuation of white confidence within society.

Instilling Fear in Black Individuals

Conversely, media representations frequently perpetuate racial stereotypes that instill fear in black individuals. Black characters are often portrayed as criminals, aggressors, and threats, perpetuating narratives of danger, deviance, and otherness. These stereotypes contribute to a climate of fear and suspicion surrounding black individuals, shaping societal perceptions and interactions.

Moreover, the sensationalization of crime and violence in media often perpetuates negative associations with blackness, contributing to the pervasive fear of black individuals within society. The overrepresentation of black individuals in news stories related to crime and violence reinforces a narrative of fear and distrust, perpetuating the marginalization and stigmatization of black communities.

Impact on Societal Perceptions and Attitudes

The pervasive nature of these media representations has a profound impact on societal perceptions and attitudes towards race. White individuals are often socialized into a world that affirms their worth and capabilities, while black individuals contend with the burden of negative stereotypes and societal suspicion. These contrasting portrayals contribute to the perpetuation of racial hierarchies and power dynamics, shaping the experiences of confidence and fear within society.

Furthermore, media representations influence not only individual attitudes but also institutional practices and policies. The perpetuation of racial stereotypes in media contributes to the normalization of discriminatory practices within various societal institutions, including law enforcement, education, and employment, perpetuating disparities in opportunities and outcomes along racial lines.

Challenging Media Narratives and Promoting Representation

It is essential to critically engage with and challenge the dominant media narratives that perpetuate racial stereotypes and contribute to the reinforcement of confidence in white individuals and fear in black individuals. By promoting diverse and inclusive representations in media, society can work towards dismantling the pervasive impact of these stereotypes and fostering a more nuanced and affirming understanding of race.

Additionally, media creators and industry professionals have a responsibility to critically examine the ways in which their work contributes to the perpetuation of racial stereotypes and to actively work towards more equitable and authentic representations of diverse experiences.

The perception is media portrayals play a significant role in shaping societal perceptions of race and reinforcing racial stereotypes, contributing to the perpetuation of confidence in white individuals and fear in black individuals. By critically examining the impact of media narratives on perceptions and attitudes towards race, society can work towards challenging the dominant narratives and promoting more positive change.

Chapter 5

Economic Systems and World Power

The topic of global economic systems and their historical connections to racial dominance is complex and multifaceted. Throughout history, various economic systems have indeed been intertwined with the dynamics of power and race, often resulting in patterns that have favored certain racial groups over others. Here are some key points to consider when examining this issue:

1. Colonialism and imperialism: Historically, European powers engaged in colonialism and imperialism, establishing economic systems that exploited the resources and labor of non-white populations in Africa, Asia, the Americas, and other regions. This exploitation often reinforced racial hierarchies and contributed to the accumulation of wealth in European nations at the expense of colonized peoples.

2. Slavery and the transatlantic slave trade: The transatlantic slave trade and the institution of slavery played a significant role in shaping global economic systems, particularly during the colonial era. The forced labor of enslaved Africans contributed to the economic development of European colonies in the Americas, while also

entrenching racial hierarchies and power imbalances.

3. Legacy of inequality: The legacies of colonialism, imperialism, and slavery have had enduring impacts on global economic systems. Even after the formal end of colonial rule and the abolition of slavery, the effects of these historical injustices continue to shape patterns of economic inequality, access to resources, and the distribution of power along racial lines.

4. Contemporary manifestations: Today, while overt colonialism and slavery have been abolished, the effects of historical racialized economic systems persist. Racial disparities in wealth, income, and access to economic opportunities are evident in many parts of the world, reflecting deep-seated historical patterns of exploitation and marginalization.

5. Intersection with confidence and fear dynamics: The historical privileging of white dominance within global economic systems has contributed to the perpetuation of confidence among white populations and fear among non-white populations. This dynamic is rooted in historical experiences of exploitation, marginalization, and

the enduring legacy of racialized economic inequality.

In understanding the intersection of economic systems and racial dynamics, it is crucial to acknowledge the historical context and the enduring impacts of past injustices. Addressing these issues requires a comprehensive approach that encompasses economic policy, social justice initiatives, and a commitment to confronting and redressing historical inequalities. Addressing the intersection of economic systems and racial dynamics requires a multifaceted approach that takes into account historical context, ongoing structural inequalities, and the need for systemic change. Here are some additional points to consider:

1. Redefining economic systems: Efforts to address historical patterns of racial dominance in global economic systems require a reevaluation of economic structures and policies. This includes examining the ways in which economic institutions and practices may perpetuate racial inequalities and working towards creating more inclusive and equitable economic systems.

2. Empowerment and opportunity: Initiatives aimed at addressing racial disparities in economic power should prioritize the empowerment of marginalized communities and the creation of opportunities for

economic advancement. This can include targeted support for minority-owned businesses, investment in education and skills training, and policies that promote inclusive economic growth.

3. Reparative justice: Many advocates argue for the need to address historical injustices through reparative measures, which may include restitution for past harms, investment in communities affected by historical exploitation, and the acknowledgment of the ongoing impacts of systemic racism on economic opportunities and outcomes.

4. Global perspective: Recognizing the global nature of economic systems and racial dynamics is essential. Efforts to address racial inequalities in economic power should take into account the interconnectedness of countries and regions, as well as the ways in which international trade, investment, and development policies can either exacerbate or alleviate racial disparities.

5. Education and awareness: Promoting understanding and awareness of the historical connections between economic systems and racial dominance is crucial. This includes incorporating discussions of these issues into educational curricula, fostering dialogue within communities,

and amplifying the voices of those directly affected
by racialized economic inequalities.

6. Policy reform: Meaningful change also requires
    policy reform at local, national, and international
    levels. This may involve enacting anti-
    discrimination laws, implementing affirmative
    action programs, and promoting diversity and
    inclusion in economic decision-making bodies.

By addressing the historical legacies of racial dominance
within economic systems and working towards more
equitable and inclusive approaches to economic
development, societies can take steps towards redressing
past injustices and building a more just and sustainable
future for all.

Chapter 6

Psychological Impacts of Racial Inequality

The psychological Impacts of racial inequality have been the focus of extensive research, shedding light on the ways in which systemic racism and inequality can affect the mental health and self-perception of individuals from both white and black communities. Here are some insights from psychological research on this topic:

1. Mental health disparities: Studies have consistently shown that individuals from racial and ethnic minority groups, including black individuals, often experience disparities in mental health outcomes compared to white individuals. These disparities can manifest in higher rates of depression, anxiety, post-traumatic stress disorder, and other mental health conditions among minority populations.

2. Racial trauma: Psychological research has highlighted the concept of racial trauma, which refers to the psychological and emotional distress resulting from experiences of racism and discrimination. Racial trauma can have profound and long-lasting effects on individuals' mental health, contributing to symptoms of distress and emotional suffering.

3. Internalized racism: Psychological research has examined the phenomenon of internalized racism, which refers to the internalization of negative racial stereotypes and beliefs about one's own racial group. Both black and white individuals can internalize racial biases, which can have detrimental effects on self-esteem, self-worth, and mental well-being.

4. Perceived discrimination: Studies have explored the impact of perceived discrimination on mental health. Perceived discrimination, whether based on race, ethnicity, or other factors, has been linked to increased psychological distress, lower self-esteem, and a range of negative emotional outcomes.

5. Intersectionality: Psychological research has increasingly recognized the importance of understanding the intersection of race with other social identities, such as gender, sexual orientation, and socioeconomic status. Intersectional approaches to studying the psychological impacts of racial inequality provide insights into the unique experiences and challenges faced by individuals with multiple marginalized identities.

6. White identity and privilege: Research has also examined the psychological implications of white identity and privilege. For many white individuals,

confronting issues of racial inequality and privilege can lead to feelings of guilt, defensiveness, or cognitive dissonance. Understanding the psychological dimensions of white identity can inform efforts to promote allyship and anti-racist action.

7. Coping strategies and resilience: Psychological research has explored the coping strategies and resilience factors that individuals use to navigate experiences of racial inequality and discrimination. This research highlights the importance of social support, community resilience, and culturally informed interventions in promoting mental well-being in the face of racial adversity.

By understanding the psychological impacts of racial inequality, researchers, mental health professionals, and policymakers can work to develop interventions and policies that address the unique needs of individuals affected by systemic racism and promote mental health and well-being across diverse communities.8. Intergenerational trauma: Psychological research has also investigated the concept of intergenerational trauma, which refers to the transmission of trauma and its psychological effects across generations. For black individuals and communities, the historical legacy of slavery, segregation, and systemic discrimination has been linked to Intergenerational trauma, impacting mental health and well-being in subsequent generations.

8. Cultural competence in mental health care: The understanding of the psychological impacts of racial inequality underscores the importance of cultural competence in mental health care. Mental health professionals must be attuned to the ways in which systemic racism and inequality can shape individuals' experiences and psychological well-being and be equipped to provide culturally sensitive and responsive care.

9. Advocacy and social change: Psychological research on the impacts of racial inequality can inform advocacy efforts and social change initiatives. By illuminating the psychological toll of racism, this research can help mobilize support for policies and interventions aimed at addressing systemic inequities and promoting mental health equity for all individuals, regardless of race or ethnicity.

10. Empowerment and resilience-building: Understanding the psychological impacts of racial inequality can also inform efforts to promote empowerment and resilience within communities affected by racism. This can include initiatives that foster a sense of community, cultural pride, and collective resilience, as well as interventions that support individuals in developing positive racial identities and coping strategies in the face of adversity.

11. Trauma-informed approaches: Psychological research has contributed to the development of trauma-informed approaches to addressing the psychological impacts of racial inequality. These approaches emphasize understanding the ways in which experiences of racism and discrimination can shape individuals' mental health, and seek to create supportive, empowering, and healing environments for those who have been affected.

By continuing to study the psychological impacts of racial inequality, researchers and practitioners can contribute to the development of interventions, policies, and practices that promote mental health and well-being in the context of systemic racism. This work is essential for fostering greater understanding, resilience, and support for individuals and communities affected by racial inequality.

Chapter 7

The Power of Privilege

In contemporary discussions of social justice and equity, the concept of privilege has emerged as a critical lens through which to understand systemic advantages and disparities. White privilege, has been the subject of extensive analysis, shedding light on the ways in which it contributes to a sense of unearned confidence and pervasive advantages within society. This chapter will provide an in-depth analysis of white privilege, exploring its manifestations, impacts, and implications for efforts to address systemic inequality.

Understanding White Privilege

White privilege encompasses the societal advantages and benefits that white individuals experience because of their race, often without being consciously aware of them. These advantages can manifest across various domains, including education, employment, housing, healthcare, the criminal justice system, and everyday interactions. White privilege is deeply rooted in historical and contemporary systems of power and oppression, shaping the lived experiences of individuals and communities.

Manifestations of White Privilege

Manifestations of white privilege are pervasive and multifaceted. In educational settings, white students often encounter more supportive and affirming environments, experience lower rates of disciplinary action, and benefit from curricula that reflect and validate their cultural experiences. In the workforce, white individuals are more likely to be hired, promoted, and compensated fairly, while also facing lower rates of unemployment and underemployment compared to their non-white counterparts. In the criminal justice system, white individuals are less likely to be profiled, arrested, or receive harsh sentences, reflecting the systemic biases that perpetuate racial disparities.

Unearned Confidence and Systemic Advantages

White privilege contributes to a sense of unearned confidence among white individuals, as they navigate a world that systematically affirms and privileges their racial identity. This unearned confidence is rooted in the knowledge that one's race is not a barrier to accessing opportunities, resources, and fair treatment. It can manifest in the form of greater self-assuredness, comfort in social interactions, and an expectation of being heard and respected.

Furthermore, white privilege confers systemic advantages that shape life outcomes and opportunities. These advantages are embedded in societal structures and institutions, perpetuating unequal access to resources, power, and influence. From economic mobility to political representation, white individuals benefit from systemic advantages that reinforce their social and economic standing. This perpetuates a cycle of privilege, as advantages are passed down through generations, contributing to enduring disparities.

Impacts of White Privilege

The impacts of white privilege are far-reaching and intersect with various aspects of individuals' lives. For white individuals, the experience of privilege can lead to a limited awareness of the challenges faced by non-white individuals, as well as a lack of understanding of the systemic nature of racial inequality. This can contribute to a sense of entitlement and a resistance to acknowledging and addressing privilege, perpetuating a status quo that disadvantages non-white individuals.

Conversely, for non-white individuals, the impacts of white privilege are often felt in the form of systemic barriers, discrimination, and the psychological toll of navigating a society that systematically advantages whiteness. This can lead to feelings of alienation, injustice, and disempowerment, as well as the internalization of racial biases and stereotypes.

Implications for Addressing Systemic Inequality

Understanding and addressing white privilege is essential for efforts to dismantle systemic inequality. This requires a commitment to confronting the ways in which privilege operates within societal structures and institutions, as well as fostering empathy, allyship, and solidarity across racial lines. Acknowledging and challenging privilege is a crucial step in promoting equity and justice.

Implications for Addressing Systemic Inequality (continued)

Addressing white privilege also necessitates a reexamination of societal norms, policies, and practices that perpetuate racial disparities. This includes implementing anti-racism initiatives in education, employment, and criminal justice, as well as advocating for inclusive representation and decision-making. It also involves creating spaces for critical dialogue and reflection on the ways in which privilege shapes individual experiences and societal structures.

Moreover, addressing white privilege requires an investment in promoting diversity, equity, and inclusion across all sectors of society. This encompasses efforts to amplify the voices and experiences of marginalized communities, dismantle systemic barriers to opportunity, and create environments that affirm the dignity and worth of all individuals, regardless of race.

Ultimately, addressing white privilege is integral to advancing a vision of society that upholds the principles of fairness, justice, and equality. This involves a collective commitment to challenging inequitable power dynamics, dismantling systemic biases, and fostering a culture of accountability and allyship.

White privilege exerts a profound influence on societal structures, individual experiences, and efforts to address systemic inequality. By understanding the manifestations and impacts of white privilege, as well as its implications for social change, individuals and communities can work towards building a more just and equitable society for all.

Addressing white privilege requires a commitment to self-reflection, education, and advocacy, as well as a willingness to engage in uncomfortable conversations about privilege, power, and systemic inequality. It also necessitates a recognition of the ways in which privilege operates within societal institutions and a dedication to dismantling barriers to equity and justice.

By acknowledging and addressing white privilege, individuals and communities can contribute to the creation of a more inclusive, empathetic, and equitable society, where the impacts of systemic inequality are actively challenged and transformed. This requires a sustained and collective effort to confront privilege, advocate for justice, and create opportunities for all individuals to thrive, regardless of race or ethnicity.

In conclusion, understanding and addressing white privilege is essential for building a society that promotes equality, justice, and dignity for all individuals. Through intentional efforts to dismantle systemic biases and foster inclusivity, individuals and communities can work towards a future where the impacts of privilege are mitigated, and where systemic inequality is actively challenged and transformed.

Chapter 8

The Cycle of Fear

The cycle of fear within black communities is a complex and deeply rooted phenomenon shaped by generational trauma and ongoing experiences of discrimination. This chapter will delve into the mechanisms through which fear is perpetuated within black communities, examining the historical context, psychological impacts, and societal implications of this pervasive cycle.

Generational Trauma and Historical Context

The cycle of fear within black communities is intricately connected to the legacy of generational trauma stemming from centuries of systemic oppression, including slavery, segregation, and institutionalized racism. The historical context of violence, dehumanization, and social marginalization has left a profound imprint on the collective consciousness of black communities, shaping their experiences, and perpetuating intergenerational trauma.

The enduring impact of historical trauma is evident in the transmission of fear, anxiety, and hypervigilance across generations. The narratives of survival, resilience, and resistance in the face of systemic oppression have been interwoven into the fabric of black communities, contributing to a shared awareness of the pervasive threat of discrimination and violence.

Ongoing Discrimination and Systemic Inequities

The cycle of fear is perpetuated by ongoing experiences of discrimination and systemic inequities that disproportionately affect black communities. From racial profiling and police brutality to disparities in healthcare, education, and employment, black individuals continue to face pervasive barriers to safety, well-being, and opportunity.

The persistent manifestations of racism and discrimination contribute to a heightened state of fear and vigilance within black communities. This includes the fear of unjust treatment by authorities, the fear of experiencing violence or harassment, and the fear of being marginalized and overlooked within societal institutions. These fears are not unfounded, as they are grounded in the lived experiences and historical realities of systemic injustice.

Psychological Impacts of Fear

The cycle of fear has profound psychological impacts on individuals within black communities. Chronic exposure to fear and stress can lead to heightened levels of anxiety, hypervigilance, and trauma-related symptoms. The pervasive sense of vulnerability and threat can also contribute to feelings of powerlessness, hopelessness, and a diminished sense of safety within one's own community and broader society.

Furthermore, the cycle of fear can manifest in the form of intergenerational transmission of anxiety and hypervigilance. Parents and caregivers may pass on a heightened awareness of threat and a need for protective behaviors to their children, perpetuating a cycle of fear that spans across generations.

Societal Implications and Consequences

The perpetuation of fear within black communities has far-reaching societal implications. It contributes to the erosion of trust in societal institutions, including law enforcement, healthcare, and education, as well as a heightened sense of alienation and marginalization. The cycle of fear can also impact community cohesion, social mobility, and the ability to fully engage in civic and economic life.

Moreover, the cycle of fear intersects with broader narratives and stereotypes about black individuals, contributing to the perpetuation of stigmatizing beliefs and biases. This can further entrench systemic inequities and perpetuate a cycle of fear-based responses within societal institutions.

Breaking the Cycle: Healing and Empowerment

Breaking the cycle of fear within black communities requires a multifaceted approach that addresses the underlying sources of trauma and systemic injustice. This involves fostering healing, resilience, and empowerment within black communities, as well as advocating for systemic change to dismantle the structures that perpetuate fear and inequality.

Chapter 9

Education as a Battleground

In the modern world, education serves as a critical battleground where disparities in opportunities and outcomes significantly influence the prospects and self-confidence of individuals. These disparities, often rooted in socioeconomic, cultural, and institutional factors, can have profound and lasting effects on the lives of students, shaping their trajectories and opportunities for success. This chapter will explore the multifaceted nature of educational disparities, their impact on individuals, and the broader implications for society.

At the heart of the issue lies the unequal distribution of educational resources and opportunities. Across the globe, students from disadvantaged backgrounds often face limited access to high-quality schools, experienced teachers, and essential learning materials. As a result, they are at a significant disadvantage compared to their more privileged counterparts. These disparities can manifest in various ways, including variations in academic achievement, graduation rates, and access to post-secondary education. The implications of such disparities are far-reaching, as they can perpetuate cycles of poverty and inequality, limiting the potential of entire communities and societies.

Moreover, educational disparities can have a profound impact on students' self-confidence and sense of worth.

When individuals are consistently exposed to environments where resources are scarce, opportunities are limited, and expectations are low, their self-perception and aspirations are inevitably shaped by these experiences. As a result, many students from disadvantaged backgrounds may internalize a sense of inferiority and develop a diminished belief in their own capabilities. This phenomenon is particularly concerning, as it can lead to a self-fulfilling prophecy, where lower expectations result in poorer performance, further entrenching the cycle of educational disadvantage.

The consequences of educational disparities extend beyond the individual level, influencing broader social and economic dynamics. Research has shown that unequal access to education correlates with higher rates of unemployment, lower earning potential, and reduced social mobility. This perpetuates a cycle of poverty and limits the overall economic productivity of a society. Furthermore, educational disparities can contribute to social fragmentation and disenfranchisement, as marginalized groups face barriers to full participation in the social, political, and economic spheres of their communities.

Addressing educational disparities requires a multifaceted approach that encompasses policy interventions, institutional reforms, and societal shifts. At the policy level, governments and educational authorities must prioritize the equitable distribution of resources, ensuring that all students have access to high-quality education, regardless of their background. This may involve targeted investments in schools serving disadvantaged communities, initiatives to attract and retain skilled teachers in underserved areas, and the provision of comprehensive support services to address the diverse needs of students.

Furthermore, educational institutions must actively work to create inclusive learning environments that foster the academic and personal growth of all students. This entails implementing culturally responsive teaching practices, promoting diversity in curricula, and providing targeted support for students from underrepresented backgrounds. By recognizing and valuing the unique strengths and experiences of each student, educators can help cultivate a sense of belonging and self-efficacy, thereby mitigating the negative impact of educational disparities on students' self-confidence.

Beyond policy and institutional reforms, societal attitudes and perceptions regarding education must also undergo a transformation. It is crucial to challenge stereotypes and biases that perpetuate unequal opportunities for different groups of students. By promoting a culture of high expectations and support for all learners, regardless of their background, communities can contribute to leveling the playing field and empowering individuals to reach their full potential.

In conclusion, education serves as a critical battleground where disparities in opportunities and outcomes profoundly influence the future prospects and self-confidence of individuals. The multifaceted nature of educational disparities underscores the need for a comprehensive and concerted effort to address this issue. By recognizing the far-reaching impact of educational disparities and taking proactive steps to mitigate their effects, societies can create more inclusive and equitable educational systems that better serve the needs of all students.

It is important to emphasize that addressing educational disparities is not only a matter of social justice but also a pragmatic investment in the future. By providing all individuals with the opportunity to receive a high-quality education, societies can unlock the untapped potential of countless students, fostering innovation, creativity, and economic growth. Furthermore, reducing educational disparities can contribute to the creation of more cohesive and resilient communities, where individuals from diverse backgrounds can contribute to the collective progress and well-being of society.

In conclusion, education as a battleground for disparities in opportunities and outcomes is a pressing issue that demands attention and action. By acknowledging the profound impact of educational disparities on individuals and society, and by implementing targeted interventions at the policy, institutional, and societal levels, it is possible to create more equitable and inclusive educational systems. Ultimately, by ensuring that all individuals have access to the resources, support, and opportunities they need to thrive, we can build a more just, prosperous, and harmonious future for generations to come.

Chapter 10

Representation Matters

The significance of positive representation in building confidence among black individuals and breaking down stereotypes cannot be overstated. In a world where media, literature, and popular culture play a pivotal role in shaping perceptions and attitudes, the absence or misrepresentation of black voices and experiences has far-reaching implications. This chapter will explore the critical role of representation in empowering black individuals, challenging harmful stereotypes, and fostering a more inclusive and equitable society.

Positive representation serves as a powerful tool for building confidence and self-worth among black individuals. When individuals see themselves reflected in a variety of contexts, including the media, literature, and positions of influence, it sends a powerful message that their experiences, perspectives, and contributions are valued and worthy of recognition. This validation can have a profound impact on self-esteem, helping individuals develop a strong sense of identity and agency. Moreover, positive representation can inspire young black people to aspire to new heights, providing them with role models and examples of success to emulate.

Conversely, the absence or misrepresentation of black voices can perpetuate damaging stereotypes and erode confidence. When black individuals are consistently portrayed in narrow and limiting ways, it can reinforce harmful narratives that undermine their worth and potential. This phenomenon can have a particularly detrimental effect on young people, who may internalize these negative portrayals and struggle to envision a future where they can achieve their aspirations. As a result, the power of positive representation in building confidence and self-worth cannot be overstated.

Beyond its impact on individuals, representation also plays a crucial role in breaking down stereotypes and challenging systemic biases. When black individuals are portrayed in diverse and multifaceted ways, it challenges monolithic and dehumanizing stereotypes that have long plagued perceptions of the black community. By showcasing the richness and complexity of black experiences, positive representation helps to counteract the reductive and harmful narratives that have historically marginalized and devalued black voices.

Moreover, positive representation can foster empathy and understanding among individuals from different backgrounds. When people are exposed to authentic and nuanced portrayals of black experiences, it can humanize the black community, fostering greater empathy and solidarity. By dispelling stereotypes and promoting a more accurate understanding of the diversity within the black community, positive representation can contribute to the creation of more inclusive and interconnected societies.

The Impact of positive representation extends to various spheres of life, including education, employment, and leadership. In educational settings, diverse and inclusive curricula that incorporate a range of voices and perspectives can provide students with a more comprehensive understanding of history, culture, and society. This not only benefits black students by validating their experiences but also enriches the educational experience of all students, fostering greater cultural competence and critical thinking.

In the realm of employment and leadership, positive representation is essential for breaking down barriers and creating pathways for advancement. When black individuals are represented in positions of authority, influence, and expertise, it sends a powerful message about their capabilities and potential. Moreover, diverse representation in leadership can lead to more informed decision-making, greater innovation, and improved outcomes for organizations and society.

The Importance of positive representation in building confidence among black individuals and breaking down stereotypes underscores the need for deliberate and sustained efforts to promote inclusivity and diversity in all aspects of society. This requires proactive measures to amplify black voices and experiences across various platforms, including media, the arts, education, and the workforce. Furthermore, it necessitates the dismantling of systemic barriers that perpetuate unequal access to opportunities and representation. Efforts to promote positive representation should begin with a commitment to inclusivity and equity in media and popular culture. This entails supporting and showcasing a diverse range of creators, artists, and storytellers who can authentically convey the breadth of black experiences. By providing platforms and opportunities for black voices to be heard, seen, and celebrated, media and cultural institutions can play a transformative role in shaping perceptions and attitudes.

Moreover, the promotion of positive representation requires a critical examination of existing structures and practices that perpetuate inequality. This includes addressing disparities in the entertainment industry, publishing, and other creative fields, where black creators and professionals continue to face barriers to entry and advancement. By fostering more inclusive and equitable environments, these industries can cultivate a rich tapestry of voices and narratives that resonate with diverse audiences.

In educational settings, the integration of diverse perspectives and histories into curricula is essential for promoting positive representation and challenging stereotypes. This involves revising and expanding educational materials to ensure that they reflect the contributions and experiences of black individuals throughout history and in contemporary society. By providing students with a comprehensive understanding of the world, educators can foster empathy, critical thinking, and a deep appreciation for the richness of human experiences.

In the workplace, efforts to promote positive representation should focus on creating inclusive environments that value and support the contributions of black professionals. This includes implementing diversity and inclusion initiatives, mentorship programs, and leadership development opportunities that empower black employees to thrive and advance in their careers. Furthermore, organizations must prioritize equitable hiring practices and create pathways for underrepresented individuals to access leadership roles, ensuring that diverse voices are represented at every level of decision-making.

Beyond these specific measures, promoting positive representation requires a broader cultural shift that challenges entrenched biases and actively confronts systemic inequities. This necessitates ongoing dialogue and collaboration between individuals, communities, and institutions to dismantle barriers and cultivate a more inclusive society. By confronting and addressing the root causes of inequality, societies can create the conditions for positive representation to flourish and for all individuals to feel valued, respected, and empowered.

In conclusion, the importance of positive representation in building confidence among black individuals and breaking down stereotypes cannot be overstated. By amplifying diverse voices, challenging harmful narratives, and fostering empathy and understanding, positive representation has the power to transform perceptions, attitudes, and opportunities. It is a crucial component of creating a more equitable, inclusive, and just society—one where all individuals, regardless of their background, can see themselves reflected in the stories we tell, the images we see, and the opportunities we pursue. By championing positive representation, we can create a world where every individual is valued, celebrated, and empowered to reach their full potential.

Chapter 11

The Role of Leadership

Examining the role of leadership within communities and at the national level in reinforcing or challenging the status quo of racial dominance reveals the profound influence that leaders wield in shaping societal attitudes, policies, and power dynamics. Leadership, whether exercised by individuals, institutions, or movements, plays a pivotal role in either perpetuating systems of racial dominance or in effecting transformative change towards equity and justice. This chapter will explore the complexities of leadership in the context of racial dynamics, examining how it can serve as a force for either reinforcing or challenging the status quo.

At the community level, leadership often emerges from within social, cultural, and civic structures, where individuals assume roles of influence and authority. Within racially diverse communities, leadership can manifest in various forms, including community organizers, religious leaders, activists, and grassroots advocates. The actions and decisions of these leaders can significantly impact the dynamics of racial dominance within their communities.

Leadership within communities can reinforce the status quo of racial dominance through inaction, complicity, or perpetuation of discriminatory practices. When leaders fail to address systemic inequalities, uphold discriminatory traditions, or prioritize the interests of dominant racial groups over marginalized communities, they effectively perpetuate the existing power imbalances. In such cases, leadership becomes a tool for maintaining the status quo, entrenching racial hierarchies, and inhibiting progress towards genuine equity and inclusion.

Conversely, community leaders can challenge the status quo of racial dominance by actively advocating for justice, equity, and systemic change. Through their words, actions, and initiatives, these leaders can mobilize their communities to confront racial injustice, dismantle discriminatory practices, and advocate for the rights and dignity of marginalized groups. By fostering dialogue, promoting education, and organizing collective action, these leaders can serve as catalysts for transformative change within their communities, disrupting established power dynamics and advancing the cause of racial equality.

At the national level, political leaders, policymakers, and public figures hold significant influence in shaping the narratives, laws, and institutions that govern society. The actions and decisions of national leaders can either reinforce or challenge the status quo of racial dominance, thereby shaping the trajectory of progress towards racial equity.

National leadership can reinforce the status quo of racial dominance through policies, rhetoric, and actions that perpetuate systemic inequalities and uphold structures of privilege. When leaders fail to address issues of racial injustice, implement discriminatory policies, or engage in divisive and prejudiced rhetoric, they contribute to the perpetuation of racial dominance. In doing so, they undermine the potential for meaningful progress towards a society where all individuals are treated with fairness, dignity, and respect.

Conversely, national leaders can challenge the status quo of racial dominance by championing policies and initiatives that promote equity, inclusivity, and justice. Through legislative action, executive orders, and public advocacy, these leaders can address systemic inequalities, combat discrimination, and work to dismantle institutional barriers that perpetuate racial dominance. By using their platforms to amplify the voices of marginalized communities, advocate for inclusive policies, and promote dialogue on issues of race and equity, national leaders can play a pivotal role in effecting meaningful change.

In addition to formal political leadership, cultural and thought leaders also hold significant sway in shaping societal attitudes and norms. Writers, artists, intellectuals, and public figures who use their platforms to challenge prevailing narratives, amplify underrepresented voices, and advocate for social change can profoundly impact the discourse on race and racial dominance. By offering alternative perspectives, fostering empathy, and challenging entrenched biases, these leaders can contribute to a more nuanced and inclusive understanding of racial dynamics, inspiring others to question the status quo and work towards a more just and equitable society.

The role of leadership in reinforcing or challenging the status quo of racial dominance is not merely a matter of individual actions, but also of the broader systems and structures in which leaders operate. In many cases, leaders are constrained or empowered by institutional frameworks, historical legacies, and prevailing cultural norms. Therefore, addressing racial dominance requires a comprehensive approach that encompasses both individual leadership and systemic change.

Efforts to challenge racial dominance and promote equity require leaders to engage in critical self-reflection, acknowledging their own biases and privileges, and committing to ongoing learning and growth. By cultivating cultural competence, empathy, and a deep understanding of the complexities of race and power, leaders can adopt more inclusive and equitable approaches to their roles, fostering environments where all individuals are valued and empowered.

Furthermore, leaders must actively work to dismantle systemic barriers and advocate for policies and practices that address the root causes of racial dominance. This may involve implementing affirmative action measures, promoting diversity and inclusion in hiring and representation, and investing in programs that address the specific needs of marginalized communities. By leveraging their influence and resources, leaders can drive systemic change that fosters greater equity and opportunity for all individuals.

In the realm of public discourse, leaders have a responsibility to foster dialogue and understanding around issues of race and racial dominance. By engaging in honest and respectful conversations, leaders can create spaces for diverse perspectives to be heard, challenging entrenched narratives, and fostering empathy and solidarity. This requires leaders to actively listen to the experiences of those affected by racial dominance, amplify their voices, and work towards building bridges across racial divides.

Leadership in challenging racial dominance also necessitates a commitment to coalition-building and collective action. Leaders must work to build alliances across racial, ethnic, and cultural lines, recognizing that efforts to combat racial dominance require the engagement and support of individuals from all backgrounds. By fostering solidarity and collaboration, leaders can create a powerful force for change that transcends divisions and works towards a more equitable and inclusive society.

In conclusion, the role of leadership in reinforcing or challenging the status quo of racial dominance is a complex and multifaceted phenomenon that encompasses individual actions, institutional dynamics, and broader societal contexts. Leaders at the community and national levels have the potential to either perpetuate existing systems of racial dominance or to effect transformative change towards equity and justice. By acknowledging their influence, committing to self-reflection, and learning, and advocating for systemic change, leaders can play a pivotal role in shaping a future where racial dominance is dismantled, and all individuals are afforded dignity, respect, and opportunity.

Chapter 12

Activism and Community Resilience

In the face of systemic oppression and fear, black communities have a long history of resistance and resilience, often rooted in a deep sense of unity and a commitment to social justice. This chapter explores the stories and strategies of activism and community resilience that have emerged within black communities, countering the pervasive systems of fear and oppression.

One of the most powerful forms of resistance within black communities has been the cultivation of a strong sense of identity and culture. Despite centuries of attempts to erase their history and marginalize their contributions, black communities have consistently reaffirmed their cultural heritage through art, music, literature, and other forms of expression. These cultural expressions serve as a source of strength and resilience, providing a platform for storytelling, healing, and the preservation of traditions. By celebrating their cultural identity, black communities have been able to resist the dehumanization and erasure perpetuated by systems of fear and oppression.

Black activism has played a vital role in challenging systemic injustices and advocating for meaningful change. From the Civil Rights Movement to the Black Lives Matter movement, black activists have organized and mobilized communities to demand an end to racial discrimination, police brutality, and other forms of institutionalized oppression. Through protests, advocacy, and grassroots organizing, black communities have been at the forefront of driving social and political change, inspiring resilience, and hope in the face of adversity.

In addition to activism, black communities have demonstrated remarkable resilience through their commitment to education and empowerment. Despite disparities in access to quality education, black individuals and organizations have worked tirelessly to create opportunities for learning and skill development within their communities. By prioritizing education, black communities have empowered themselves to challenge stereotypes, pursue upward mobility, and break the cycle of systemic oppression. Educational initiatives, mentorship programs, and community-based learning centers have served as powerful tools for equipping future generations with the knowledge and skills needed to thrive in the face of adversity.

The establishment of support networks and communal spaces has been instrumental in fostering resilience within black communities. Whether through churches, community centers, or grassroots organizations, these spaces serve as pillars of strength, offering emotional support, resources, and a sense of belonging. Within these networks, individuals find solidarity, mentorship, and opportunities for collective action, creating a sense of community resilience that transcends the challenges imposed by systemic fear and oppression.

Importantly, the preservation of black history and the recognition of ancestral wisdom have been central to the resilience of black communities. By acknowledging the struggles and triumphs of their ancestors, black individuals have drawn inspiration and guidance from the resilience of those who came before them. This connection to history serves as a source of empowerment, reinforcing a legacy of strength and resistance that continues to shape the identity and resilience of black communities today.

The stories and strategies of resistance and resilience within black communities stand as a testament to the enduring spirit and determination of individuals who have faced generations of systemic fear and oppression. Through cultural affirmation, activism, education, community support, and a deep connection to their history, black communities have demonstrated an unwavering commitment to overcoming adversity and creating a more just and equitable society. The resilience of these communities serves as a powerful reminder of the strength that can emerge from solidarity, collective action, and a steadfast belief in the possibility of a better future.

Chapter 13

Toward a More Equitable Society

The pursuit of a more equitable society requires a comprehensive reevaluation of existing policies and practices to dismantle systems of dominance and build a society based on equity and mutual respect. This chapter delves into the discussion of policies and practices that could bring about meaningful change and foster a society where all individuals have equal opportunities and are treated with dignity and fairness.

At the core of this pursuit lies the need for transformative policies that address systemic inequalities across various domains, including education, employment, healthcare, criminal justice, and housing. In the realm of education, for instance, equitable funding mechanisms and resources must be implemented to ensure that all students, regardless of their background, have access to high-quality education and the support they need to succeed. This may involve redistributing resources to schools in underprivileged communities and addressing disparities in educational outcomes through targeted interventions.

Similarly, in the realm of employment, policies aimed at eliminating workplace discrimination, promoting diversity and inclusion, and ensuring fair wages are essential to fostering equity. This may involve implementing affirmative action programs, strengthening anti-discrimination laws, and encouraging corporate transparency and accountability in hiring and promotion practices. Additionally, measures to address wage gaps and provide pathways for career advancement for marginalized communities can contribute to a more equitable employment landscape.

In the realm of healthcare, establishing universal access to affordable, high-quality healthcare is paramount for building an equitable society. This may involve implementing universal healthcare systems, expanding access to preventive care and mental health services, and addressing disparities in health outcomes among different demographic groups. By ensuring that all individuals have access to comprehensive healthcare, regardless of their socioeconomic status or background, society can take a significant step toward equity in health outcomes.

Furthermore, reforming the criminal justice system is crucial for dismantling systems of dominance and advancing equity. This may involve reevaluating sentencing guidelines, addressing mass incarceration, promoting alternatives to incarceration, and implementing restorative justice practices. Additionally, efforts to address racial and socioeconomic disparities in policing and the legal system, as well as promoting rehabilitation and reintegration for formerly incarcerated individuals, are integral to creating a more just and equitable society.

In the realm of housing, policies aimed at addressing housing discrimination, promoting affordable housing, and combating residential segregation are essential for fostering equity. This may involve implementing fair housing laws, expanding affordable housing initiatives, and investing in community development to create inclusive and diverse neighborhoods. By addressing housing disparities and promoting access to safe and affordable housing for all, society can work toward dismantling systemic barriers to housing equity.

In addition to policy reforms, fostering a more equitable society requires a shift in institutional practices and cultural norms. This includes promoting diversity and inclusion in all sectors, dismantling implicit biases, and creating opportunities for meaningful dialogue and understanding across diverse communities. By actively challenging discriminatory practices and fostering a culture of mutual respect and empathy, society can begin to unravel the deeply ingrained systems of dominance that perpetuate inequality.

Centering the voices and experiences of marginalized communities in decision-making processes is essential for creating policies and practices that truly reflect the needs and aspirations of all individuals. This may involve promoting representation and leadership from diverse backgrounds in government, businesses, and civil society, as well as actively engaging communities in participatory decision-making processes. By prioritizing inclusivity and empowerment, society can build a foundation for equity that is rooted in the lived experiences and aspirations of its diverse population.

The journey toward a more equitable society necessitates a multifaceted approach that combines transformative policies and practices with a commitment to challenging entrenched power dynamics and fostering a culture of mutual respect and understanding. By addressing systemic inequalities in education, employment, healthcare, criminal justice, and housing, society can begin to dismantle systems of dominance and create pathways for equity and justice for all individuals.

Prioritizing diversity, inclusion, and representation across all sectors is crucial for reshaping institutional practices and cultural norms. This entails actively confronting implicit biases, promoting anti-discrimination measures, and creating spaces for meaningful dialogue and collaboration among diverse communities. By fostering a culture that values and celebrates diversity, society can work towards dismantling the barriers that perpetuate inequality and exclusion.

Additionally, the pursuit of a more equitable society requires an ongoing commitment to listening to and uplifting the voices of marginalized communities. This involves centering the experiences and perspectives of those who have been historically marginalized and advocating for their inclusion in decision-making processes. By amplifying these voices and actively involving them in shaping policies and practices, society can cultivate a more inclusive and responsive approach to governance and social change.

Building a more equitable society necessitates a collective commitment to dismantling systemic barriers and creating opportunities for all individuals to thrive. This requires a sustained effort to address the intersections of race, gender, class, ability, and other forms of identity-based discrimination, recognizing that equity can only be achieved through an intersectional lens that acknowledges the complexities of individual experiences and challenges.

Ultimately, the journey toward a more equitable society is an ongoing process that demands collective action, empathy, and a willingness to confront and transform systems of dominance and inequality. It calls for a reimagining of policies, practices, and cultural norms to create a society where every individual is valued, empowered, and afforded equal opportunities to reach their full potential.

The pursuit of a more equitable society requires a holistic approach that encompasses policy reforms, institutional change, cultural transformation, and a steadfast commitment to amplifying the voices of marginalized communities. By addressing systemic inequalities and dismantling systems of dominance, society can work towards creating a future where equity, mutual respect, and justice are fundamental principles that guide governance, social interactions, and collective well-being. This vision of a more equitable society is one that acknowledges the inherent worth and dignity of every individual and strives to create a world where all are empowered to thrive and contribute to the common good.

Chapter 14

Healing and Reconciliation

The wounds of racial division run deep, leaving lasting scars on individuals and communities. Healing these wounds and building bridges between communities requires a thoughtful and deliberate process that acknowledges historical injustices, fosters empathy, and promotes meaningful dialogue. This chapter explores the necessary steps for healing the wounds of racial division and advancing reconciliation between communities.

At the heart of healing and reconciliation lies the acknowledgment of historical injustices and their enduring impact on individuals and communities. This involves recognizing the legacies of slavery, colonization, segregation, and systemic discrimination that have contributed to racial divisions and inequities. By acknowledging these historical injustices, society can begin to confront the painful truths of the past and work towards a more inclusive and equitable future.

Fostering empathy and understanding is essential for building bridges between communities. This entails creating opportunities for individuals to listen to and learn from the experiences of others, particularly those who have been historically marginalized or oppressed. Through empathy-building initiatives, storytelling, and cultural exchange, communities can develop a deeper understanding of the diverse perspectives and experiences that shape the lived realities of others.

In addition, promoting meaningful dialogue and truth-telling is fundamental to the process of healing and reconciliation. This involves creating spaces for open and honest conversations about the impact of racial division, systemic injustices, and personal experiences of discrimination. By providing platforms for dialogue, communities can engage in truth-telling that acknowledges the pain and trauma caused by racial division while also seeking paths toward healing and understanding.

The pursuit of healing and reconciliation requires a commitment to restorative justice practices that center the needs of affected communities. Restorative justice emphasizes accountability, healing, and repairing harm, rather than punitive measures alone. By prioritizing restorative justice, communities can work towards addressing the root causes of racial division and fostering healing in a manner that acknowledges the dignity and humanity of all individuals involved.

Additionally, creating opportunities for collaborative action and mutual support is integral to the process of healing and reconciliation. This involves fostering partnerships between diverse communities to address shared challenges, promote social cohesion, and advance common goals. By working together on initiatives that promote equity, justice, and community well-being, individuals and communities can build trust and solidarity, laying the foundation for genuine reconciliation.

Promoting education and awareness is essential for fostering healing and reconciliation. This includes integrating the histories and experiences of marginalized communities into educational curricula, promoting cultural competency, and providing opportunities for individuals to learn about the diverse contributions of different communities. By fostering a deeper understanding of diverse cultural backgrounds and histories, society can work towards building empathy and dismantling stereotypes that perpetuate racial division.

Creating spaces for healing and cultural expression is crucial for fostering resilience and promoting reconciliation. This may involve supporting community-based healing initiatives, arts and cultural programs, and commemorations that honor the experiences and contributions of diverse communities. By providing spaces for healing and cultural expression, communities can affirm the value of diverse identities and promote a sense of belonging and inclusion.

Healing the wounds of racial division and advancing reconciliation between communities requires a multifaceted approach that prioritizes acknowledging historical injustices, fostering empathy, promoting meaningful dialogue, and centering restorative justice practices. By creating opportunities for collaborative action, promoting education and awareness, and providing spaces for healing and cultural expression, society can work towards building bridges between communities and fostering a future characterized by empathy, understanding, and mutual respect. This vision of healing and reconciliation is one that acknowledges the pain of the past while seeking to create a more just and inclusive future for all individuals and communities.

It is essential to recognize the role of leadership and advocacy in driving the process of healing and reconciliation. Leaders at all levels of society, including political, religious, and community leaders, have a responsibility to promote healing, reconciliation, and social cohesion. This involves actively engaging in efforts to address racial divisions, advocating for policies that promote equity and justice, and modeling respectful and inclusive behavior.

Fostering healing and reconciliation requires a commitment to ongoing truth-telling and addressing contemporary manifestations of racism and discrimination. By acknowledging and addressing systemic injustices, such as disparities in access to education, healthcare, and economic opportunity, society can work towards dismantling the structural barriers that perpetuate racial division.

Promoting intercultural understanding and solidarity is vital for building bridges between communities and fostering reconciliation. This may involve creating opportunities for intercultural exchange, promoting multicultural events and initiatives, and supporting efforts to celebrate the diversity of communities. By recognizing and celebrating the richness of diverse cultural traditions, society can promote a sense of collective belonging and shared humanity.

Ultimately, the journey toward healing and reconciliation is a collective endeavor that requires ongoing commitment, empathy, and a willingness to confront the legacies of racial division. By prioritizing truth-telling, empathy, restorative justice, and collaborative action, communities can work towards healing the wounds of the past and building a future characterized by understanding, solidarity, and mutual respect.

In conclusion, the pursuit of healing and reconciliation is a vital step towards creating a society where individuals and communities can overcome the legacies of racial division and work towards a future characterized by empathy, understanding, and social cohesion. Through acknowledging historical injustices, promoting meaningful dialogue, and fostering restorative justice practices, society can foster healing and reconciliation, ultimately building bridges between communities and advancing a vision of a more just, equitable, and inclusive future for all.

Chapter 15

A Call to Action: Embracing a Shared Future

This final chapter would serve as a motivational call to action, encouraging all readers to take personal responsibility for dismantling the systems that perpetuate racial dominance. It would outline concrete steps that individuals can take, such as engaging in open dialogue, educating themselves and others, supporting black-owned businesses, advocating for policy changes, and participating in community outreach. This chapter would emphasize the importance of collective effort and solidarity in creating a society where confidence and emotional resilience are accessible to all, regardless of race.

As we conclude this journey of exploration into the complexities of racial dominance and the pursuit of healing and reconciliation, we are reminded that the responsibility for creating a more just and equitable society rests with each one of us. It is a call to action that demands our collective effort, empathy, and unwavering commitment to dismantling the systems that perpetuate racial dominance and building a future where all individuals can thrive with confidence and emotional resilience, regardless of race.

To embrace a shared future, it is imperative that we take personal responsibility for driving meaningful change in our communities and beyond. This begins with engaging in open dialogue that acknowledges the realities of racial division and fosters empathy and understanding. By actively listening to the experiences of others, particularly those who have been marginalized, we can begin to cultivate a deep sense of empathy and solidarity that is essential for dismantling systemic barriers.

In addition to dialogue, education is a powerful tool for challenging misconceptions and dismantling systems of dominance. By educating ourselves and others about the historical and contemporary manifestations of racial injustice, we can work towards creating a more informed and empathetic society. This may involve reading literature by diverse authors, learning about the experiences of marginalized communities, and seeking out opportunities for cultural exchange and learning.

Furthermore, supporting black-owned businesses and initiatives is a tangible way to contribute to the economic empowerment of black communities. By intentionally seeking out and patronizing black-owned businesses, we can help create opportunities for economic growth, entrepreneurship, and community development. This act of support not only fosters economic resilience within black communities but also contributes to the broader movement for equity and justice.

Advocating for policy changes is another critical avenue for driving systemic transformation. This may involve engaging with local and national policymakers, participating in advocacy campaigns, and supporting initiatives that seek to address systemic inequalities in education, healthcare, criminal justice, and employment. By amplifying our voices and advocating for policy changes that promote equity and justice, we can drive meaningful systemic change.

Additionally, participating in community outreach and service is a powerful way to foster solidarity and bridge divides. By actively engaging in community initiatives, volunteering our time, and supporting grassroots organizations that work towards social justice and racial equity, we can contribute to building a more cohesive and inclusive society. This may involve mentoring youth, participating in community clean-up efforts, or supporting initiatives that promote cultural exchange and understanding.

Ultimately, the call to action is a collective endeavor that demands our individual and collective commitment to dismantling systems of dominance and creating a society where confidence and emotional resilience are accessible to all, regardless of race. It requires us to recognize the interconnectedness of our shared future and to actively work towards building a world where every individual is valued, empowered, and afforded equal opportunities to thrive.

In conclusion, the call to action is a reminder that each one of us has a role to play in creating a more just, equitable, and inclusive society. By engaging in open dialogue, educating ourselves and others, supporting black-owned businesses, advocating for policy changes, and participating in community outreach, we can contribute to the collective effort of dismantling systems that perpetuate racial dominance. Through our individual and collective actions, we can work towards a future characterized by empathy, understanding, and solidarity—a future where confidence and emotional resilience are accessible to all, regardless of race. Let us embrace this call to action with determination, empathy, and a steadfast commitment to creating a world where all individuals are equal.

The conclusion would tie together the main points from each chapter, reinforcing the central thesis of the book. It would reiterate the importance of recognizing and challenging the systems that teach confidence to white people and instill fear in black people. The conclusion would provide a hopeful outlook on the potential for change, stressing that while the road ahead is long, every step toward dismantling these constructs is a stride toward a more just and balanced world.

This book provides a framework for discussing the complex and often uncomfortable topic of racial dominance and the conditioning of confidence and fear. It aims to be thought-provoking and educational, challenging readers to examine their own beliefs and roles within societal systems and to become active participants in the movement for racial equality and justice.

www.ingramcontent.com/pod-product-compliance
Lightning Source LLC
Chambersburg PA
CBHW051914250726

48659CB00002B/646